Wit and Humour Based on Anecdotal Evidence

Wit and Humour Based on Anecdotal Evidence

Continuing the family legacy of storytelling based on my Grandfather's Anecdotes

Aparna Joshi

GYAN

Published, 2021

Published by

Gyan Publishing House
5, Ansari Road
Daryaganj, New Delhi-110002
Phone: 011-47034999, 9811692060
www.gyanbooks.com
E-mail: books@gyanbooks.com

Printed at: Gyan Press, Delhi.

Cataloging in Publication Data—DK
Courtesy: D.K. Agencies (P) Ltd. <docinfo@dkagencies.com>

Joshi, Aparna, 2002- **author.**
Wit and humour based on anecdotal evidence : continuing the family legacy of storytelling based on my grandfather's anecdotes / Aparna Joshi.
pages cm
Includes bibliographical references.
ISBN 9788121220125

1. Puri, R. K., 1938- —Anecdotes. 2. Puri, R. K., 1938- —Humor. 3. India—Kings and rulers—Anecdotes. 4. India—Kings and rulers—Humor. 5. Government executives—India—Anecdotes. 6. Government executives—India—Humor. I. Title.

LCC DS481.A1J67 2021 | DDC 954.0099 23

Dedicated to Lockdown spent in Covid times that allowed me to write down these stories often related by my Grandfather; those that were thus far unrecorded.

Contents

PART II

PRESIDENTS, PRIME MINISTERS & VISITING DIGNITARIES

Acknowledgement

I would like to thank my grandfather for indulging me and letting me document his stories and anecdotes. My grateful thanks to a very dear family friend, Ms. Ann Morrow, a former journalist with the Daily Telegraph, London, author of several books on the British Royal Family and Highness: the Maharajas of India, for her guidance and encouragement. I would also like to thank my esteemed family members, Lt.Gen. Nirbhay Sharma and Dr. D.P. Pande for constantly encouraging my grandfather to write a book and charging me with the responsibility to keep reminding him. This acknowledgement would not be complete without thanking my parents, Vibhas and Shobha Joshi. My father for his patience and unstinting support and my mother for being my constant friend, philosopher and guide.

My thanks also go to Mrs. Minakshi Watts, for her contribution in editing this book.

I would also like to thank the librarians at Delhi Gymkhana Club and India International Centre who helped me find relevant reading material for the historical introductions to each section.

Late Mr. Kishan Puri
Chief Secretary of Rajasthan
(30-12-54 — 12-1-57)
Photo Credit: Govt. of Rajasthan

Prologue

Anecdotage is a Sign of Dotage

The Cambridge Dictionary defines an anecdote as a short amusing story involving a particular person or event.

Each generation has its share of anecdotal and apocryphal tales based on amusing and endearing incidents from the lives of the famous and the obscure, from the historical personages to anonymous individuals, narrated by their contemporaries and handed down from one generation to another.

The historical accuracy of anecdotes cannot be easily vouchsafed. The tales gather more spice and flavour as they are handed down by the storyteller to the listener. As an old Italian adage goes, 'Old wine and friends improve with age!'

My generation, too, had its share of apocrypha. Some of these were myths gathered by youth, a few I was witness to.

Lest these be lost to posterity, and with no claim to originality or authenticity, my grand daughter Aparna Joshi meticulously compiled royal, political, historical and social anecdotes. Sources, where available, have been cited. For the rest, she has been guided by the adage 'Next to the originator of a good sentence is the one who quotes it.'

I owe the caption of this prologue to my father, late Mr. Kishen Puri, a raconteur of anecdotes which he would share with me and would often, with a glint in his eyes, remark,

'Anecdotage is a sign of dotage.'

Mr. R.K. Puri

Mr. R.K. Puri

Photo Credit: Ms. Lindsay Hebberd

Introduction

'There is no greater agony than bearing an untold story inside you.' – ***Maya Angelou***

My intention through this book is to pen down the stories related by my grandfather Mr. R.K. Puri, those that I have grown up on and would like to document from both an intellectual and entertaining perspective.

My grandfather's anecdotes bring to life people with stoic exteriors as people, rather than cardboard figures. He had the opportunity of personally interacting with many of these personalities as the son of the First Chief Secretary of unified Rajasthan, Mr. Kishan Puri (term 30.12.54 – 12.1.57)

Born in September 1938, my grandfather grew up during the British Raj, educated at the prestigious Mayo College in Ajmer, and post- graduation from the University of Rajasthan. A champion debater, squash and tennis player, it gave him the unique all-round exposure as a young man in the formative years of India as a Republic.

A career bureaucrat, my grandfather joined the Indian Police Service (IPS) in 1961 and Indian Railway Traffic Service (IRTS) in 1962. He was deputed to the Army Headquarters during the 1971 war. Later he represented the Ministry of Commerce and Industry, as a delegate to various International Conferences of UNECAFE and UNESCAP and Multi-lateral Trade meetings. He was also India's signatory to the First Multi-Lateral Trade Agreement between ESCAP countries- the Bangkok Agreement, on 31st July, 1975. He later served as Director, Tea Promotion, London, for UK, Ireland and Scandinavian countries.

On returning to India, my grandfather conceptualised and launched the Palace-on-Wheels in 1982, a unique tourist train similar to the legendary Istanbul-Calais Coach, popularly called the Orient Express. The Palace-on-Wheels is a tourist train created with the luxuriously re-furbished personal royal salons of the Rajas and Maharajas of 21 Indian Princely states for tourists to experience the royal lifestyle. As Founder Director of the Indian Institute of Tourism and Travel Management and Member Secretary of the National Committee on Tourism, he superannuated as Additional Member from the Railway Board.

Thereafter, he has been engaged in the formation and development of the Hotel Association of India for the past three decades.

When not working, he enjoys reading and teaching me, his 18-year old granddaughter, the usage and skill of the English language......just as his father had done for him.

I hope you enjoy the book!

Aparna Joshi

Timeline of Events

1526- Establishment of the Mughal Empire

1556- Akbar is Crowned Emperor, Aged 13

1567- Siege of Chittor

1568- Siege of Ranthambore

1576- Battle of Haldighat

1707- Death of Aurangzeb

1765- Diwani Rights of Bengal

1799- Declaration to Paramountcy

1848- Doctrine of Lapse

1857- First Revolt of Independence

1857- End of the Mughal Empire

1903- Berar Under British Rule

1911- Delhi Durbar

1918- Treaty of Versailles

1931- Shimla Pact is Signed

1939- World War II Begins

1945- World War II Ends

1947- Lord Mountbatten appointed the Viceroy of India

1947- India declared Independent

1947- Partition of India is Announced

1947- Kashmir Accedes to India

1955- Bulganin Travels to India

1956- Kwame Nkrumah visits India

1962- Sino - India War

1962- Cuban Missile Crisis

1964- Death of Jawaharlal Nehru

1965- Indo-Pak War

1966- Tashkent Agreement, Death of Lal Bahadur Shastri

1967- Devaluation of Indian Rupee

1969- Split in the Congress

1970- Abolition of Privy Purses

1971- Bangladesh War

1975- Emergency imposed

1977- Emergency withdrawn

1979- Janata Party comes to power

1980- Indira Gandhi elected from Chikmangalur

1984- Indira Gandhi Assassinated

Commissions and their History

1942- Stafford Cripps Mission

The Stafford Cripps Mission came to India with the intent of creating electorates.

1950- Planning Commission

The Planning Commission was established in 1950 with the goal of creating Five Year Plans for the development of India, Post-independence.

1951- Election Commission

The Election Commission was established in order to plan and execute the largest election in the country since 1952. The first Chairperson was Sukumar Sen.

1953- States Reorganisation Commission

The States Reorganisation Commission, was established in order to reorganise the state boundaries. It consisted of H.N. Khunzoo, Fazal Ali, K.M. Panikkar.

1977- Shah Commission

The Shah Commission was established to examine the excesses committed by the government during the Emergency. It was chaired by Justice J.C. Shah.

1979- Mandal Commission

The Mandal Commission was established in 1979, to look into the Other Backward Classes. It was chaired by B.P. Mandal.

1984- Sarkaria Commission

The Sarkaria Commission was established in 1984 to examine the Centre-State relations and it was chaired by Ranjit Singh Sarkaria.

1992- Liberhan Commission

The Liberhan Commission was established in order to resolve the dispute of the Babri Masjid. It was chaired by M.S. Liberhan.

United Nations ESCAP

The UNESCAP was the Commission that was responsible for the Economic and Social Commission for Asia Pacific. It is one of the six Regional Commissions of the UN.

Some Important Abbreviations

IPS- Indian Police Service

UNESCAP- United Nations Economic, Social Commission of the Asia Pacific

UAE- United Arab Emirates

INC- Indian National Congress

GCB- Grand Commander of the Bath

IRTS- Indian Railway Traffic Service

SRC- States Reorganisation Commission

J&K- Jammu and Kashmir

NAM- Non-Aligned Movement

USSR- Union of Soviet Socialist Republics

TBI- Tea Board of India

UoI- Union of India

PVC- Param Vir Chakra

VC- Victoria Cross

BCE- Before Common Era

CE- Common Era

Based on Anecdotal Evidence
A Synopsis

The book is a unique compilation by the author, Aparna Joshi, of tales of wit, humour and repartees, both ancient and contemporary. All inherited from the raconteurs of her family, her great grandfather, late Mr. Kishan Puri, and grandfather, Mr. R.K. Puri. Both of them served as senior civil servants in the period preceding and succeeding the independence of India.

The author has industriously compiled the incidents and events, humorous, satirical and witty in a variety of spheres such as Princes, politicians, diplomats, civil servants, army, eccentricities and incongruities of life.

The author has meticulously preserved the remembrance of persons great or small, fierce or gentle in ways that are recalled, amidst smiles and happiness such as when Mountbatten held discussions only on Mondays with Gandhi, when he observed a Maun Vrat (silence) or when Winston Churchill left an unpaid debt at the Bengaluru Club. Or, when a young Capt. Manekshaw (later Field Marshal), lying wounded on the battlefield, told the army surgeon that a mule had kicked him.

Other anecdotes include a Bard's strange homage that intrigued Akbar, the iconic song that brought tears to Nehru's eyes, the Vicereine who coveted jewellery, satires of legal luminaries like Moti Lal Nehru, Mohammad Ali Jinnah, Earl of Birkenhead in an English Court and Field Marshal Lord Montgomery's midnight misdemeanour at a Mumbai club.

The anecdotes about these personalities are remembered and narrated with fondness and affection.

Part I: The Rajas and Maharajas

While reading through the treasure trove of anecdotes held within the pages of this section, it would be useful to gain some perspective on the period of time, the geography of the region, 356 Indian states and the political systems thus established.

There is an anecdote, set in Jaipur, when the Maharaja of Jaipur travelled from India to the Continent and carried the holy water of the Ganges with him for religious reasons. Jaipur was a large and influential Principality with a number of resources and a unique rapport with the British administration.

Junagarh was a small but powerful Principality in the Saurashtra region of India. Saurashtra consists of what we now, know, as Gujarat, Maharashtra, Goa and parts of Karnataka. The Nawab of Junagadh had an obsession for dogs and celebrated the wedding of two of his favourite canines with great pomp and show, declared a State holiday and invited all citizens to the wedding feast.

The grandiose lifestyle of Indian royalty, the pomp and circumstance surrounding them is the stuff of legends. The anecdote 'The 9 Steps of Falaknuma' tells the story of the time one such ceremony was broken...the story of the accession of Hyderabad.

Jammu and Kashmir, the Jewel in India's crown has had a turbulent yet riveting history. This crown jewel has been like the Kohinoor, illusive, precious and the pride of its bearer. Many a nation have fought over the control of this jewel, but it acceded to India and 'Heaven on Earth' is the Story of India's First Param Vir Chakra.

The Durbar of 1911, was the time when King George V and his Queen, Mary visited India for an inspection of their realm. The last chapter of this section deals with stories from this Durbar, especially how the Gaekwad of Baroda defied the imperial protocol.

Part II: Presidents, Prime Ministers and Foreign Dignitaries

This part of the book deals with the post-independent India, at the time when the Second World War had ended and the Cold War was reaching its peak.

There were a few defining moments for Asia and Africa at this time, as new nations such as Pakistan were formed and the cold war led to proxy wars among the two power blocs, United States of America and the Union of Soviet Socialist Republics (USSR).

As Prime Minister of the United Kingdom, Winston Churchill, declared, 'An iron curtain has descended over Europe'.

India, Egypt, Ghana, Indonesia and Yugoslavia seized this power vacuum and laid the foundation of the Non-Aligned Movement in order to promote peace and sovereignty in the newly decolonised territories. Some of the aims of NAM are:

- Maintenance of Sovereignty
- Maintenance of territorial integrity
- Rapid Economic Development

This is popularly referred to as 'the third way' or 'NAM'.

In India too, this was truly a turbulent time, because, between 1947-71, India fought three wars with Pakistan and one war with China.

The 1960s, often known as the 'Troubled Decade' saw the deaths of two incumbent Prime Ministers, Jawaharlal Nehru in 1964, Lal Bahadur Shastri in 1965. An internal split between the Congress party in 1969 and the devaluation of the Indian rupee in 1967. Between 1975-77 the state of India's democracy was also in peril, with the imposition of the Emergency.

The Indian Foreign Policy too, witnessed a few changes

Under the leadership of Jawaharlal Nehru and Lal Bahadur Shastri, there was a steady centrist policy with the introduction of the planned developmental steps. However, under the leadership of subsequent Prime Ministers in India, a steady Soviet tilt was seen.

Some of the anecdotes connected with the global leaders who visited India after independence are captured in this book and need a special mention.

Soviet Prime Minister Khrushchev and Communist Party leader Bulganin, who visited in the 1950s, were over awed by the huge masses gathered to welcome them. They declined to travel in an open top Rolls Royce and preferred to ride in a secure prison van. 'Panchsheel'(5 principles) agreement was launched by Nehru and Chou En Lai. A visiting West Asian monarch, to India, when asked to comment on it, responded by saying, 'I have not met her yet'. He had met two or three Indian women named Sheela but not Panchsheel!

The Greek King who came on a state visit was greeted by India's Vice President, Dr. Radhakrishnan as the first Greek King to come as our honoured guest. The last one, Alexander the Great, had come uninvited.

These and many more political anecdotes enumerated in the book reflect their humane aspect.

The last part of the book contains brief biographies of those featured in the book, a bibliography, photo credits and acknowledgements.

Maps

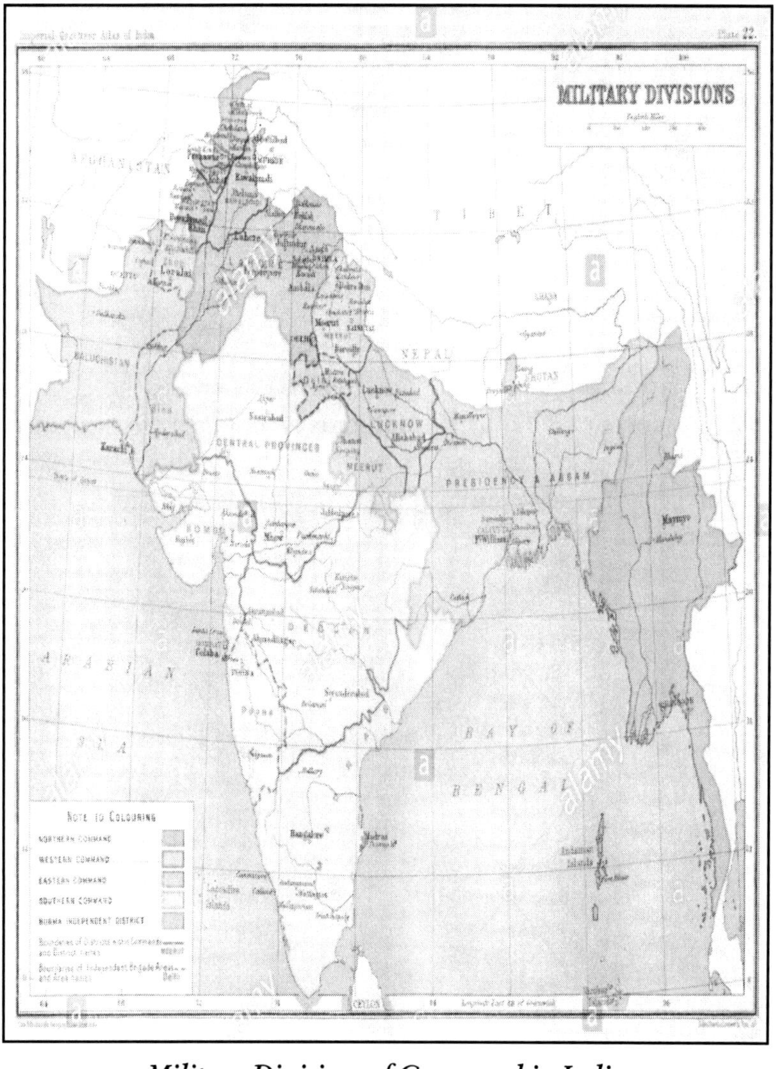

Military Divisions of Command in India

Photo Credits: Open source

Historical Introduction

While reading through this section of the book, the treasure trove of anecdotes held within the pages of this section, it would be useful to gain some perspective on the period of time, the geography of the region, 356 Indian states and the political systems thus established.

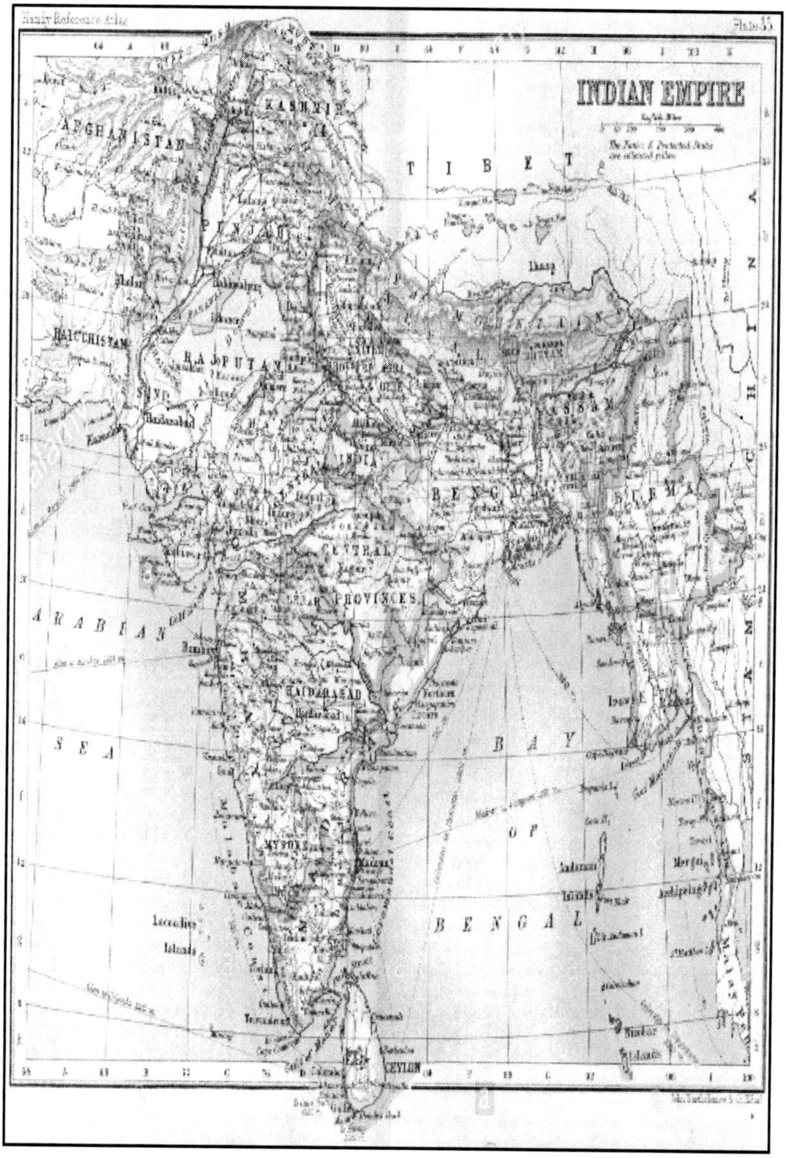

British India

Photo Credit: Open source

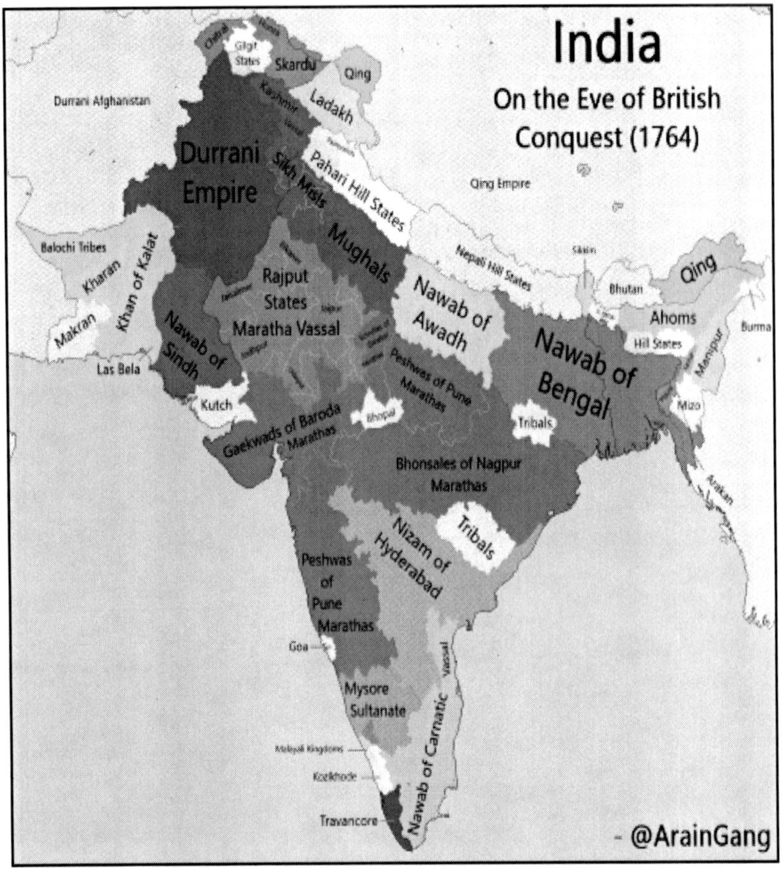

Empires of India before British Raj

Photo Credit: Pinterest

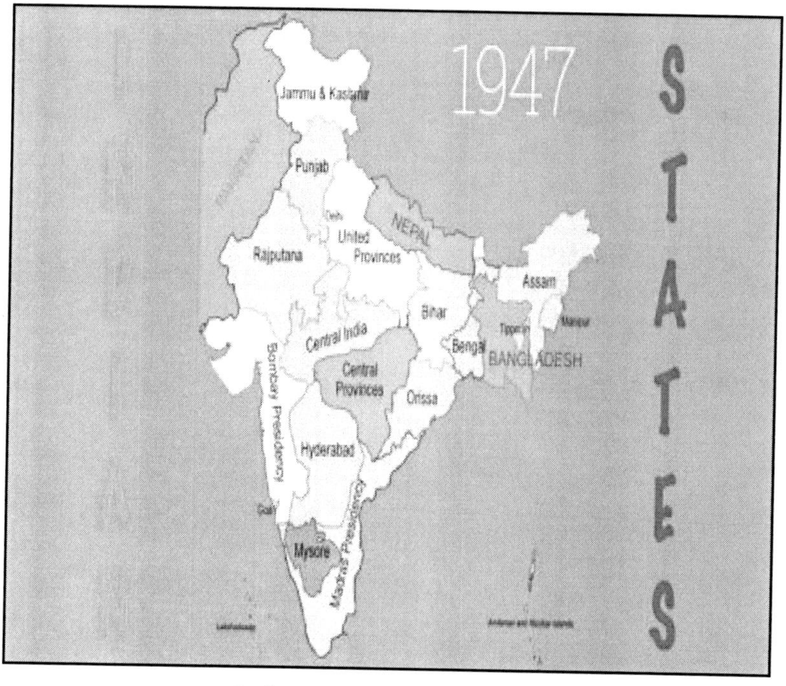

Indian Political Map 1947

Photo Credits: Quora

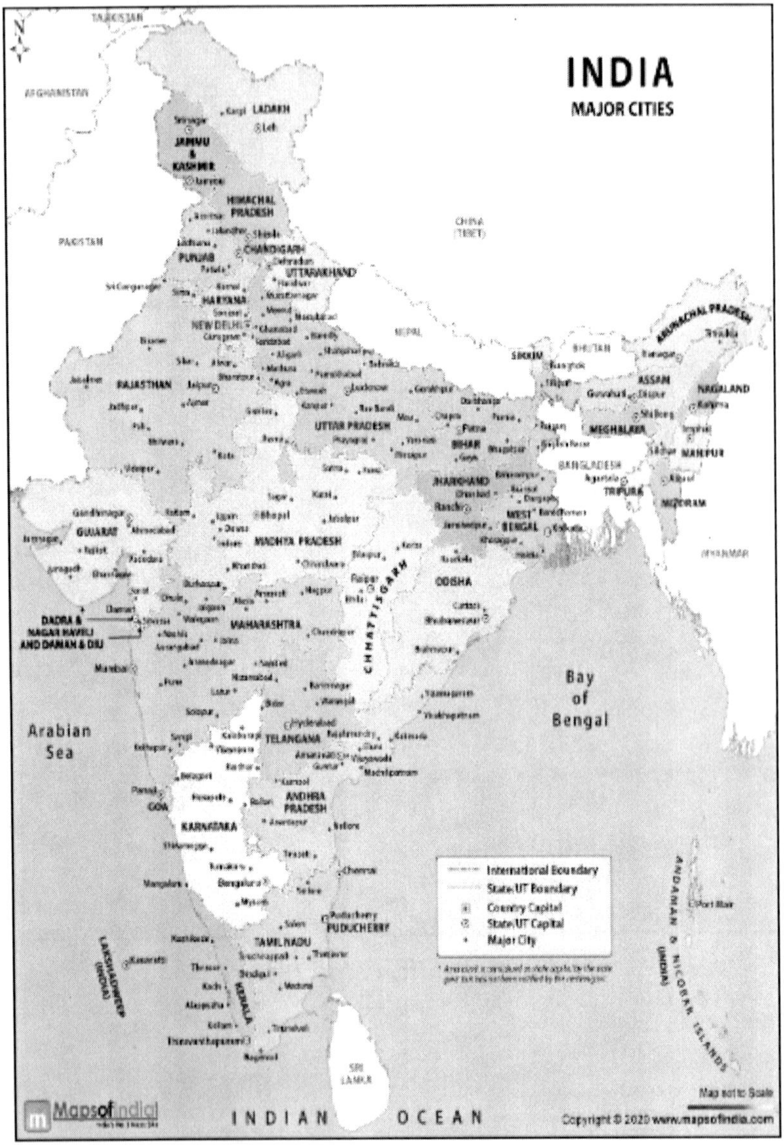

Indian Map, 2019

Photo Credits: Amazon.com

And the Scene was Set...

We all have our favourite memories of childhood, a favourite toy, place, colour or dress. Mine are ageless memories of my grandfather's stories. He has stories for all occasions, witty, humourous or the sombre. They would often be narrated with a glint in his eyes and a thoughtful smile on his face. If the house were a theatre, the Drawing room was the centre stage, and he the 'Javed Khan' (a fictional character created by Ruskin Bond) of our family. In the words of Ruskin Bond, "Those cold winter evenings as the darkness deepened", a cup of tea and stories of Princes & Princely states were the candles that added glow and warmth.

Allow me to be your 'Javed Khan' Ruskin Bond's fictional character, to explore my world through our drawing room into the 364 Princely states with their many fascinating Royal families.

Dramatis Personae

Sir Ganga Singh

1880-1943

He held various honorary titles such as the GBE, KCB, GCVO among others. He was the only non-white member of the war cabinet, therefore, he was present at the signing of the Treaty of Versailles.

Maharaja Madho Singh

He was also known as Sawai Madho Singh. The Maharaja held various titles including GCSI,GCIE and GCVO. Along with this, he held an LLD from the University of Edinburgh. In order to receive these titles, he had to often travel across four seas to Europe, putting his caste purity in jeopardy. The second chapter deals with his unique solution.

Sir Muhammad Mahabat Khan III Khanji

1911-1948

He was famous for his love of dogs and was always surrounded by them. He was also famous for his efforts to modernise Junagarh along British Lines. During the Accession process, the Nawab spent a year on holiday in Europe. In his absence, his Dewan, Sir Shah Nawaz Bhutto lobbied with Jinnah in order to merge with Pakistan. As a result of this, the Nawab spent his final years in exile.

Nizam Mir Osman Ali Khan

1886-1967

The Nizam of Hyderabad was also honoured with various titles such as GCSI, GBE. He was famous for his opulent lifestyle, sprawling palaces and the strange customs that he followed. For another interesting anecdote head over to my You Tube channel.

Maharaja Hari Singh

1895-1961

He was the Maharaja of Kashmir and was honoured by the British with various titles including GCSI, GCIE and GCVO. Maharaja Hari Singh was the last ruling monarch of Jammu and Kashmir and played a decisive role in the accession of Kashmir to India. For another anecdote from the Maharaja's multifaceted life, please head on over to my You Tube channel.

Maharaja Sayaji Rao Gaekwar III

1875-1939

The most striking part of this Maharaja's title is that his name is written in the Maratha Nomenclature (for further information head to my YouTube Channel). This is because the dynasty traced its lineage to the Maratha Empire of Deccan India. He was known for his patriotic fervour and various British and Persian titles attached both as prefixes and suffixes. These included Farzand-i-khas-i-Daulat-i-Inglishia, Khas Khel Shamsher Bahadur, GCSI, GCIE, KIH. He greatly modernised Baroda along the lines of British development and authored a book titled *'Notes on the Famine Tour'*.

Lady Mary Curzon

1870-1906

She was the wife of Lord Curzon, he held office between 1898-

1911. He held titles such as KG, GCSI, GCIE, PC, FBA. She was famous for her interest in jewellery and she was the main character in the story, 'The Vicereine and the Ring'. For more interesting anecdotes about Lady Curzon. Head yet again to my You Tube channel.

Maharaja Jaswant Singh Rathore

1629-1678

He was honoured with the title 'Mirza Raja'. He was sent on the military campaign to Afghanistan, where he felt like an outsider after the familiar surroundings of Jodhpur, where he was the Subedar. To get a taste of the story in the original language, follow up video in my grandfather's voice on my You Tube channel.

Maharana Pratap I

1540-1597

He was one of the earliest rulers of Mewar. He was considered a local hero for his valour in the face of Mughal infiltration of Marwar and Mewar. There are many stories that captured the imagination of the masses that included him and his gallant steed Chetak. A story and a voice over video with these stories is available at my YouTube channel.

King George V

1865-1936

King George V of England is probably one of the most recognisable figure heads in the world today. His face appears on the coins of the United Kingdom. He is most famous for attending the Delhi Durbar with his wife Queen Mary of England. He also attempted to broker peace with India and provide for independence. His death led to world wide speculation and intrigue in the royal family, with one of the most famous abdications in British history, post the famous speech of Queen Elizabeth I. "I have the heart and stomach of a man, a King of England."

Maharaja Jai Singh Prabhakar

1882-1937

The Maharaja of Alwar was popular for his erudite and effervescent nature. He was honoured by the British with the titles of GCSI, GCIE. He was known in the British aristocracy for his lavish lifestyle and love for fine jewellery. He was also a keen polo player and architect. The Maharaja built the Sariska Lodge that is today a luxury hotel belonging to the Taj Group.

For other stories head to my YouTube Channel 'Based on Anecdotal Evidence'.

Part I

THE RAJAS AND MAHARAJAS

1

Travelling with the Holy Ganges

'One does not discover new lands without consenting to lose sight of shore for a very long time.' – **Andre Gide**

India was governed by a complex system of social class and order that regulated all interactions between people. Way back in the 19th and 20th centuries, people believed that foreign waters, visiting foreign lands and contact with foreign people could damage their caste purity.

This incident relates to an extremely caste conscious Maharaja of Jaipur, Maharaja Madho Singhji. He was expected to travel to London for the Coronation of King Edward VII of England in 1902. Being a devout Hindu, he agreed to travel after consulting his astrologers. There were two conditions.

Firstly, his retinue must include an Indian Brahmin cook to prepare his meals.

Secondly, he be allowed to carry the water of the Holy Ganges to drink and purify himself on his return journey, having crossed the seven seas.

He was allowed both his conditions. However, there lay logistical challenges in the transportation of river water. When this was brought to his notice, the Maharaja ordered the making of two large vessels of sterling silver, weighing 345 kg, 1.6 meters in height, with the capacity to hold 4000 litres of Ganges water.

The largest pair of vessels, recognised by the Guinness Book of Records, can be seen standing tall at the City Palace of Jaipur as a memento of Jaipur's vibrant history.

Ganges Water Vessel, City Palace Jaipur

Photo Credits: British Broadcasting Corporation (BBC)

2

For the Love of Dogs

'Dogs are not our whole lives but they make our lives whole.'
*– **Roger. A. Caras***

The Indian subcontinent is filled with folklore and stories about the pursuit of exotic wildlife and the extravagant lives pets of royalty may have led. Another example of an equally pampered pet is in the stories of Garfield.

When we comb through the pages of Indian history, we find an Indian Nawab to whom dogs deserved the same status as humans.

The Nawab of Junagarh was famous for his adulation for his canine companions. He would celebrate their birthdays and even arranged for his favourite dog's wedding in a similar manner as the Hindu wedding ceremonies. The 'groom' side carried in decorated palanquins by liveried attendants. He declared a state holiday to enable the public to participate in the festivities.

His love for dogs almost led him to forget his wife, who was still packing, but not his dogs, while leaving India in a hurry, to board a ship to Pakistan. However, this is a matter of hear-say!

The erstwhile Nawab had wanted to accede his State to Pakistan, however, the move was quashed by the Indian armed forces.

Nawab of Junagarh with one of his 800 dogs, each of whom was bedecked with gold and silver ornaments.

Photo Credit: Tim from Open Source

3

Down the Nine steps of Falaknuma

The Falaknuma Palace, now a luxury hotel in Hyderabad, was once the residence of the most powerful Nawabs of India. (Hyderabad being one of the largest Princely states of the time.) It's architectural marvels include extensive palace grounds, the largest dining table in the world and a train to move the haute cuisine for guests, instead of the standard Lazy Suzy. This same Palace entrance is no less grand. Nine marble steps lead up to the front '*Dwar*' or doorway.

The Nawab of Hyderabad was honoured by the Colonial government with the title His Exalted Highness. He was also given the GCB and his heir apparent was known as the Prince of Berar, perhaps, akin to the Prince of Wales!

The Nawab had made it a practice to receive all guests including the Viceroy, on the ninth step of this Palace. He had also been the most reluctant to sign the Instrument of Accession, give up sovereignty and be part of the Union of India.

As a last resort, the then Home Minister of India, Sardar Patel, decided to surround the city with the army and force the Nawab and his paramilitary force, known as the 'Razakars', into submission.

The Nawab suitably chastened by now, thought it prudent to go to the airport to receive Sardar Patel and sign the Instrument of Accession, thus, foregoing the tradition of receiving his guests on the 'ninth step' of his palace.

This story is based on folklore, it has not been proven by history.

Jawaharlal Nehru, Nawab of Hyderabad and General J. N. Choudhary

Photo Credits: The Hindu

4

This is Heaven on Earth

***'Gar Firdaus bar-roo-e (beautiful face) zamin ast,
hami ast-o, hami ast-o, hamin ast'***

'If there is heaven on Earth it is here, it is here, it is here'
– Abdul Hamid Lahori
Padshahnama

Jehangir quoted this line when he visited Kashmir. Peace however, evaded the valley after the Mughal rule. Kashmir was attacked and conquered by the Afghans. Later the British colonisation of India brought further turmoil.

As many would call it, it was a paradoxical situation. A Hindu Maharaja ruling a majority Muslim population with a minority of persecuted Kashmiri Pandits.

In October 1947, J&K was invaded by Pakistani militia, disguised as local tribals. The Maharaja who had resisted the signing of the Instrument of Accession, felt helpless and sent an urgent call for help to the Indian leaders. The brave 13 Kumaon Regiment under the leadership of Major Somnath Sharma was sent to defend J&K.

Major Somnath Sharma had one of his arms in a plaster due to an injury incurred while training. However, to keep up the morale of his unit, he personally loaded weapons and bravely defended the Motherland.

This ended in the ultimate sacrifice on his part, yet what lives on are the words from his citation :

> *"The enemy is 50 yards from us.*
> *We are heavily outnumbered. We are under devastating fire. I shall not withdraw an inch, but will fight to the last man and our last round."*
>
> **– Major Somnath Sharma**

Thus, was born India's first Param Vir Chakra, the highest Gallantry award. This award in itself has a tale to tell. A national competition was held to design the PVC. The chosen winning design was made by a Hungarian lady, who was settled in Pune. Her daughter is married to the deceased Major's younger brother.

Constitutional provisions under Article 370 integrated Jammu and Kashmir with India. In 2019, with the abrogation of these provisions, India has taken a new step towards further integration.

Major Somnath Sharma
Photo Credit: Medium.com

Maharaja Hari Singh of Jammu and Kashmir
Photo Credits: Wikimedia Commons

5

The Durbar Disasters: 1911

The Delhi Durbar of 1911 was one of the largest shows of pomp and pageantry, often compared to the tricentenary of the Romanovs.

However, for any event to be memorable, there must be a glitch. At this event, there were two that caused the Viceroy more than a few sleepless nights.

The first incident is related to a large principality in the Rajputana. The Maharaja was supposed to be awarded the Star of India, for his service to the Crown. However, he refused to accept, on grounds that his ancestors owed their lineage to the Sun God. He could not lower himself to the status of a lowly star and therefore returned from halfway enroute to Delhi.

Another story fondly related by my grandfather is about the Maharaja of a large and important principality in Gujarat. The Maharaja transgressed the regal protocol by marching up to King George V with a cane. He moved beyond the halting line. He did not wear the expected and formal ceremonial attire (siropa). He came in casual attire, did not bow to show his subordination and then turned his back on the Imperial Couple of England before returning to his position.

It smacked of arrogance in the eyes of the colonial masters but was regarded by historians as a strong gesture of dissent.

Raisina Hill Delhi Durbar 1911
Photo Credits: Wikipedia

King George V and Queen Mary of England
Photo Credits: Shutter Stock

6

The Vicereine's Dinner and the Regal Ring

'Jewellery has the power to be the one little thing that makes you feel unique.' – ***Elizabeth Taylor***

This short anecdote also deals with a Maharaja from the Rajputana region who also was extremely cautious about any physical contact with British officials. In order to maintain no contact, he always wore a pair of gloves and thus maintained his caste-class purity.

At one such formal banquet the Maharaja was wearing a very attractive ring. The Vicereine was attracted to this ring. She had a reputation for gaining small pieces of jewellery from royalty in India by complimenting it!

In this case too, she attempted the same, by complimenting the ring multiple times. However, the king did not relent. She desired to closely scrutinise the ring. In response to this request, the Maharaja removed the ring and placed it on her quarter plate. When returning the ring, the Vicereine was instructed to leave the ring on the Maharaja's quarter plate. From the quarter plate, the Maharaja proceeded to gingerly lift the ring with a fork and disinfect it in wine.

This incident of humiliating his wife infuriated the Viceroy, who instantly deposed the said Maharaja on grounds of mental instability.

7

Alone and Abandoned in the Desert

When one travels long distances away from home in unknown territories, one looks for familiarity wherever one can find it.

Such was the case with a reluctant Raja of the desert state of Jodhpur. He had been sent to Afghanistan along with Rajput warriors by Aurangzeb, the then Mughal Emperor of India, wanting to expand his Empire beyond Kabul and Kandahar. He had already made several attempts, all in vain. As the Rajput Raja was travelling in the Persian desert, he noticed a certain palm succulent, similar to ones he saw in abundance at home in Marwar. Being extremely home sick, he addressed a poetic query to the palm in his local language which translates as follows:

> "Oh! My beloved Cacti, how come thee here? Were you expelled from home like me to this forsaken terrain? In this far off desert?"

The heartbroken Maharaja Jaswant Singh, pining for his home and hearth, breathed his last on 28th December, at Jamrud, near Khyber Pass.

8

The Bard's Strange Tribute

The term 'bard' often reminds one of William Shakespeare. However, in Rajputana, as the State of Rajasthan was known in pre-Independence India, consisting of over 25 Princely states ruled by independent Rajas, there was a centuries old bardic tradition. Bards and minstrels wrote and sang verses in praise of these Rajas, reminding them of their proud lineage. The bards accompanied them in battles to sing songs of valour and the sacrifices made by their ancestors.

One such wandering bard reached Mewar where the famous Rajput warrior King Rana Pratap, had set up camp after the Battle of Haldighati. He sang songs in the praise of the Rana and his ancestors. Just having returned from the battle, and camped in a forest, the Rana had only his 'Safa,' (headgear), to give as a reward.

A few months later, the same wandering bard reached the Mughal Emperor's court and on entering, he gave the traditional tribute of 'Chaar Taslim' i.e bowing low from the waist, one arm behind and the other lifted four times to the forehead. However, this bard held the Rana's headgear high above his own head as he bowed before the Emperor to pay obeisance.

When the Emperor asked him for the reason for his peculiar greeting, the bard said,

> "Your Majesty, my head is my own and it bows to your Imperial Majesty, but this headgear is a gift from Rana Pratap, and it bows only before God."

The Emperor is said to have been struck by this response and did not pursue fighting with the Rana, turning his attention towards Gujarat and the Southern Indian states.

9

The Power of a Comma

'What is common between a cat and a comma:
A cat has claws at the end of it paws, while a comma is a pause at the end of a clause.'- *Anonymous*

I'm sure we all have distinct memories of being taught the basics of English grammar. This is the story of the Prince of Wales learning English Grammar in the presence of his father, the King. With an inquisitive expression, the King enquired, "Teacher, as an heir to this Kingdom, why must my son learn grammar like my subjects, commoners ?"

In order to dispel his confusion, the teacher picked up a piece of chalk and wrote on the board: The King said, the teacher is a fool.

The King agreed with the statement that the teacher was indeed a fool. In the following sentence, the teacher wrote to the contrary!

'The King, says the teacher, is a fool.'

On reading this, the indignant King understood the importance of grammar and told his son to study his grammar diligently.

10

Plus Fours, Minus Fours

Mahatma Gandhi was persuaded by the British Viceroy to attend the Second Roundtable Conference in September 1931, being held in London to discuss Constitutional reforms with Indian political leaders.

King George V hosted a reception at the Buckingham Palace for the delegates.

The Indian delegation was unable to persuade Gandhi to wear a formal suit to the reception.

One of the most famous reported conversations was about the dress code to be followed in the presence of the King.

Mahatma Gandhi wore a Khadi loin cloth and shawl, while the King wore his formal attire known as 'Plus Fours'.

The King was seen smilingly greeting Gandhi. On emerging from the reception, Mahatma Gandhi was surrounded by newspaper correspondents, who asked him if he had not felt underdressed while meeting His Majesty.

Gandhi is said to have replied with his toothy smile: "No, no, not at all. The King wore Plus Fours and I wore Minus Fours. Between us we are adequately dressed."

Mahatma Gandhi at 10 Downing Street

Photo Credits: Reddit

11

Gandhi's Goat in London

We have all grown up on the *Puss in Boots* poem which went as follows:

Pussy cat, Pussy cat, where have you been?
I've been to London to meet the Queen.
Pussy Cat, Pussy Cat, what did you do there ?
I frightened a little mouse under the chair!

This story is not about a cat but about the Father of the Nation.

Gandhiji was very particular about certain things in his daily routine and dietary habits.

When visiting England for the Second Round Table Conference, he had a very unique and strange request, to take his goat with him as he only drank goat's milk.

The King thought this request very strange but agreed to it.

Gandhi in London

Photo Credits: Hindustan Times

Part II

PRESIDENTS, PRIME MINISTERS & VISITING DIGNITARIES

A Magic Carpet Ride

Magical – that is the truest and most accurate word which can explain reading along with my grandfather. I recall reading a newspaper for the first time, when I was five years old and bombarding my grandfather with questions about national and world leaders, attempting to make sense of the long and often confusing names.

He often laughed at these attempts and would jovially place me on his knee, while relating anecdotes of Pandit Jawaharlal Nehru, Queen Elizabeth II or Dr. S. Radhakrishnan.

As I grew up, I began to develop a flair for reading the law and legal documents. The first document he ever made me memorise was the Preamble to the Constitution of India. This later developed into reading complex theses, spending hours in our library, in the light of a soft yellow lamp. As my grandfather watched me read, he told me stories of M.A. Jinnah, F.E. Smith and other legal luminaries to invigorate my interest.

Dear reader, in this section, allow me to be your narrator and tell you the stories that once inspired and still continue to inspire me to this day, each time I hear them, years after the first time!

The Dramatis Personae

Nikolai Alexandrovich Bulganin

1895-1975

He began his career in the Cheka or the Russian Secret Police. The progress of his working life gained more importance with the rise of Stalin as he served on the War Cabinet of 1944. At the end of the war and the beginning of the Cold War, he was appointed the Defence Minister of Soviet Russia. In this capacity, he visited India in 1955.

Nikita Sergeyvich Khrushchev

1894-1971

He was the first secretary of the Communist Party of the Soviet Union. Later, Khrushchev was elected the leader of USSR at this time he began and supported the process of destalinisation in order to liberalise the USSR. He visited India in this capacity.

Jawaharlal Nehru

1889-1964

Jawaharlal Nehru was born in 1889. He was born in Allahabad. His father was a Barrister at law from England. In his early years, he was a grassroot worker with the Indian National Congress. He was mentored by Mahatma Gandhi, this made him a popular leader among the masses. He was the first Prime Minister of India after independence.

John Glenn

He was the director and film producer of the James Bond movie, Octopussy.

12

The Russian Encounter

'If you want to control a population give them a God to worship.'
– ***Noam Chomsky***

This anecdote is about the State visit of the Soviet Defence Minister, Nikolai Alexandrovich Bulganin and Nikita Sergeyvich Khrushchev. They travelled to India in 1955. This was soon after Jawaharlal Nehru had travelled to USSR and brought to India the idea of the Planning Commission (1950).

Their aircraft landed on the Jaipur airstrip, and was welcomed by a sea of humanity. The Soviets, unfamiliar with such scenes, were taken aback by their lavish welcome as excited locals ran towards a new '*Cheel Gadi*' the name for an aircraft in local language.

However, this was not the most bizarre detail of the Soviet travel plan. The Government of India had selected an open-air car for them to be the centre piece of the motorcade. The Soviets, being sceptical of the large, unruly crowd and their safety, opted for a prison van!

This led to a thorough investigation into the failed law and order situation, which was later cleared.

Bulganin, Nehru and Nikita Khrushchev

Photo Credits: Amazon.com

13

God to the Soviets

'Communism has decided against the Bible and against all religions.' ***– Billy Graham***

This quote was proven true by an incident involving Nikita Khrushchev's government. It is reproduced below:

> 'The village administrator went to the local potato farmers to collect the annual revenue and enquired about the potato harvest that year. The farmer said that due to the grace of God, there were heaps of potatoes. The administrator replied, 'There was no God', to which the farmer responded, 'There are no heaps of potatoes either.'

Due to the inhospitable climate of Russia, potato and vodka were the two mainstays of the economy, the decline in their production spelt economic distress for the Soviet Union.

The ideal of collective farming
(A stamp from U.S.S.R.)
Photo Credits: Shutter Stock

The reality of Collective Farming
Photo credits: Quora

14

The Fruit Bill of Jawaharlal Nehru

'Live as if you were to die tomorrow, learn as if you were to live forever.' – ***Mahatma Gandhi***

This is an anecdote related to the first Prime Minister of India, Jawaharlal Nehru. Teen Murti Bhawan, the official residence of the Prime Minister had an abundance of fruit trees and vegetable gardens. The fresh produce was routinely a part of the fare at the table for the Prime Minister, his daughter Indira Gandhi and their visitors.

On a certain occasion, the Indian Revenue Department conducted its annual audit headed by a young probationer at the department. Due to his inexperience, he raised a question about the average consumption and cost of the fresh produce consumed at the head table. He also recommended an average lump sum in his final report in the audit.

This recommendation, though opposed by his immediate superiors, was however, supported by their superiors. Therefore, a bill was placed on the desk of Jawaharlal Nehru for the price of the fresh produce.

Being gracious and compassionate, Jawaharlal Nehru promptly wrote a cheque for Rs. 5000/- as payment for this bill.

This story is a reflection of the ethics and compassion of the popular leaders of those times.

The extensive grounds of Teen Murti Bhawan
Photo Credits: Daily hunt.com

15

The Octopussy Odyssey

'Bond is a rare breed soon to be extinct.'

– ***Kamal Khan***

Octopussy 1983

The quoted line is from the iconic James Bond movie that was filmed in India in 1982. Around the same time, the legendary 'Palace on Wheels' tourist train was being tested. The film director, John Glenn, approached officials for permission to shoot a decisive train chase sequence in a short two-day window, on the Palace on Wheels. It would be the ideal setting for the scene. My grandfather eagerly took the proposal to his seniors. However, due to short notice and permission being required from various ministries this golden opportunity was lost.

However, even today, when he relates the story with his ubiquitous zest, the movie becomes just a bit more memorable.

The Palace on Wheels

Photo Credits: Palace on Wheels website

16

The Scholar Ambassador of India

'Russia is a riddle, wrapped in a mystery, inside an enigma'
– *Winston Churchill*

The Cold War was a period of tension between two ideologies the open capitalist society of the USA and the closed communist society of the USSR.

Members of the international community did not have any idea about the conditions of the USSR, other than what the state propaganda said. Stalin, did not encourage diplomatic exchanges by interacting with visiting envoys either.

There was one exception though, the 'Scholar Ambassador' from India, Dr. S. Radhakrishnan.

While discussing the Cold War tensions with Stalin and the possible de-escalation, Stalin reportedly told Dr. Radha Krishnan, 'It takes two to tango.' By this he implied that both the US and the USSR should be in consensus and shake hands on a truce.

In response to this, Dr.S.Radhakrishnan said, 'If you withdraw, the US will have no option but to de-escalate.' The process of de-escalation began with the declaration of Détente, uneasy peace, in 1975 and it took another sixteen years for the Cold War to end.

Stalin and Lenin

Photo Credit: Cysaby.com

Dr. S. Radhakrishnan

Photo Credit: Cysaby.com

17

The NAM Coat

'Action to be effective must be directed to clearly conceived ends.'
– Jawaharlal Nehru

India became a Republic in truly trying times, both on the national and international stage. It was also laying the foundation of the Non-Aligned Movement to combat the Cold War tensions. To advance this agenda, Kwame Nkrumah visited India in 1957. He was scheduled to visit Srinagar from Delhi. However, being from a tropical nation, travelling to another tropical nation, he did not carry adequate woollens. Upon hearing this, Jawaharlal Nehru travelled to the Old Delhi Railway Station, clad in an oversized coat.

The Ghanaian Premier was taken aback by Nehru's presence, and commented "That coat seems to be too large for you!" Nehru responded, "It is for me, but wouldn't be for you!"

In the pockets of this coat was a pair of fur lined gloves to ward off the bitter cold of Srinagar.

Both the State visit and this act of compassion were visionary and carefully executed.

Jawaharlal Nehru and Kwame Nkrumah, Waldorf meeting, 1960

Photo credit: Historic Images outlet

18

Frost

Stopping by the Woods on a Snowy Evening,
– Robert Frost

Whose woods these are I think I know.
His house is in the village though;
He will not see me stopping here
To watch his woods, fill up with snow.

My little horse must think it queer
To stop without a farmhouse near
Between the woods and frozen lake
The darkest evening of the year.

He gives his harness bells a shake
To ask if there is some mistake.
The only other sound's the sweep
Of easy wind and downy flake.

The woods are lovely, dark and deep,
But I have promises to keep,
And miles to go before I sleep,
And miles to go before I sleep.

This iconic poem was on the bedside of Jawaharlal Nehru at his home in the hills, to remind and inspire him of his promise to the people of India.

19

Panchsheel.... who is she?

The Panchsheel Treaty was signed between India and China in 1954, bringing peace between the two countries for eight years.

Its terms were as follows:

1. Mutual co-existence
2. Mutual respect for sovereignty
3. Equality and mutual benefit
4. Mutual non-interference in each other's internal matters
5. Mutual Peace

It was a widely discussed topic among world leaders.

When the Saudi Sheikh was asked by reporters about his views on 'Panchsheel', he responded, "Who is she? we haven't been introduced."

This was because he had already met a few ladies by the name of 'Sheila' and knew it was a popular name in India!

Dr. Rajendra Prasad, Saudi Sheikh and Jawaharlal Nehru in Varanasi, 1955

Photo Credit: Wikipedia

20

Thus, the Shimla Accord came to be

'Victory belongs to the most persevering.'
– Napoleon Bonaparte

The 1971 war was a momentous event in Indian Military history due to the many tactical and climatic challenges faced by the Indian Army and Air Force. Equally, its end was also historic.

The war ended with the historic Shimla Accord. The Shimla Agreement was signed by the Indian Prime Minister Indira Gandhi and President Zulfikar Ali Bhutto on 2nd July 1972. Bhutto arrived accompanied by his young daughter, Benazir and stayed at the Raj Bhawan as state guests. At the guest house, Zulfikar Ali Bhutto's bedroom was redecorated to remove a portrait of Indira Gandhi, one she herself felt would make Bhutto ill at ease, especially as the leader of a surrendered nation.

The day the accord was signed, reporters asked Indira Gandhi, whether it was a boy or a girl. The response to this was: 'It's a boy'. This signified that the accord had been successfully inked.

Zulfikar Ali Bhutto, Indira Gandhi, Benazir Bhutto

Photo Credit: CC BY-NC-ND

21

The Cleopatra Profile

'She overcame everything that was meant to destroy her.'
– Sylvester MacNutt III

After reading the book 'One Life is not Enough,' which is an autobiography by K. Natwar Singh, a former Minister of External Affairs and senior politician of the Indian National Congress, who has also written many hitherto, unknown facts about Mrs. Indira Gandhi, my grandfather said "That is remarkable but interesting." What he meant was that Indira Gandhi, one of India's most powerful women, could have habits similar to many of us! Indira Gandhi used to draw the profile of Cleopatra on the margins of drafts. This intrigued my grandfather.

Both women of power and influence, who met tragic ends. Both of them were taken down by causes from which they could have been protected. Cleopatra died under mysterious circumstances, rumoured to have been bitten by an Egyptian Cobra. Indira Gandhi was shot dead by three shots at point blank range.

Their legends live on to this day.

Cleopatra

Indira Gandhi

22

Death of D.E.M O' Cracy

Each individual has his/her own memory of the imposition of Emergency (1975).

One of my grandfather's memories of the emergency is part limerick part pun, that appeared in a national daily. It was written by editor Ashoka Madhavan. It is reproduced below:

NOTICE

This is to announce the death of

Mr. D.E.M O'Cracy

Mourned by his wife T. Ruth,

Son L.I. Berty

Survived by his Daughters

Faith and Justice

23

My body is now Amendments

Another interesting story about the Emergency is a reported conversation between a visiting politician and Jayaprakash Narayan when he was dangerously ill in 1975.

This is how it went:

"How are you, JP?

"Well, my body is all amendments, much like the Constitution."

24

The Little Sparrow

'Experience is not what happened to you.
It is what you do with what happens to me.'
– ***Lal Bahadur Shastri***

A unique experience to recall is the signing of the Tashkent Declaration. The most distinct memory of the event for my grandfather was Tashkent Radio's description of Indian Prime Minister, Lal Bahadur Shastri, as 'The Little Sparrow'.

This was a parody for the height difference between Ayyub Khan, Alexei Kosygin and Lal Bahadur Shastri, while getting a grand welcome on the streets of Tashkent.

Ayyub Khan, Lal Bahadur Shastri and Alexei Kosygin

Photo Credits: Russian Council

25

Humour in Parliament

The British House of Commons is perhaps the most well-known repository of parliamentary humour and political sallies. A classic example is the debate between the firebrand Conservative Party leader Benjamin Disraeli and the gentle William E Gladstone, the leader of the Liberal Party.

Exasperated by Disreali's sallies, Gladstone remarked, "Dizzy, you will meet your death either at the gallows or die of some loathsome disease." Prompt came Disraeli's retort, "That would depend, my honourable friend, on whether I embrace your principles or your wife."

Winston Churchill was equally famous for his witty retorts and one liners. Once a lady member of the House of Commons, Nancy Astor, who had frequent exchanges of vitriolic sallies with Churchill, remarked, "Winston, if you were my husband, I would put poison in your coffee." Prompt came Churchill's retort, "Nancy, if you were my wife, I would drink it."

There is an apocryphal story of one of Churchill's sons-in-law, asking a loaded question at a function held to honour Churchill as the greatest leader of World War II, as to "Who, in the Prime Minister's opinion, is the greatest war time leader ?" A visibly offended Churchill glared at him and said : "Benito Mussolini." After a pause he added "because he had the guts to hang his son-in-law, Count Ciano."

In the Indian Parliament, there are very few examples of wit and humour. Late Piloo Mody, Lok Sabha member from 1967 to 1977 and Rajya Sabha member from 1978 to 1983, used to introduce humour in his own inimitable style. During a discussion on espionage activities, he entered the Parliament with a placard dangling on his shirt embossed with the words : "I am a CIA Agent."

During Question Hour when officials were required to be present in the officials gallery to furnish instant material to their ministers for replying to supplementary questions asked by MPs, Piloo Mody would send chits to Prime Minister Indira Gandhi marked to 'IG' and signed off as 'PM'. Indira Gandhi also responded in the same vein marking her notes to 'PM' and signed as 'IG' . These slips landed in the officials' gallery, sending the concerned officers into a frenzy to determine which slips were from the Prime Minister and which from Piloo Mody.

There is another instance of humour in Parliament when Indira Gandhi was asked why she did not want to meet Pakistan President Yahya Khan. She replied, "You cannot shake hands with a clenched fist."

Yet another instance of Indira Gandhi's humour outside Parliament was her reply to Peter Ustinov, a renowned English actor, writer and TV host, who while interviewing Indira Gandhi asked her why the telephones in India did not work efficiently ? Mrs. Gandhi's response was classic "They call the system Cross Bar but I think they mean Cross Wire."

Once Acharya Kriplani, the veteran leader of the Praja Socialist Party, was mounting a blistering attack on the Congress led Central Government. A member reminded him that his wife, Sucheta Kriplani, was the Congress Chief Minister of Uttar Pradesh. Acharya Kriplani, responded "So far I thought, Congressmen were only incompetent, now I know they even run away with other people's wives."

The Indian Parliament, which is based on the Westminster model of Parliament, has its members more focused on healthy debates. However, they do need to have a more liberal infusion of wit and humour, which creates bonhomie and goodwill in the House.

26

Hit by a Mule

Generals are often believed to maintain a tough personality. However, this is often an illusion. This story is from the life of General Sam Manekshaw.

A classic example of this trait is the episode related to bravery in action of Field Marshal Sam Manekshaw, M.C. As a Captain from India, he led the charge for capturing the Pagoda Hill on 4th February 1942, in Burma during World War II. He was wounded with nine bullets to his body.

At the hospital, the attending Australian surgeon asked Manekshaw, "What happened?" He responded that he had been 'kicked by a mule!' Impressed by Manekshaw, the surgeon said "By Jove! You have a sense of humour!" He operated upon him and removed the nine bullets. And Manekshaw lived to the ripe old age of 94 having been the Chief of the Indian Army, Victor of Pakistan, awardee of not only India's highest military and civilian honours but also the Military Cross.

Sam Manekshaw, a young Portrait
Photo Credits: The Quint

27

Barristers at Law

'The Golden Rule is clear: do not sound like a lawyer any more than is absolutely necessary.' – ***Keith Evans***

Barrister at Law from England is the highest and most famous law degree in India. The stories of these barristers are famous for their humour and ready wit.

This was a moment in the Indian courts before independence.

Muhammad Ali Jinnah appeared at a court carrying a large collection of books. The judge enquired why he had brought so many books, with him. To this Jinnah replied: "To teach you law My lord."

Jinnah as a Practising Barrister

Photo Credits: Dawn.com

28

The Shimla Pact and Delhi Gymkhana Club

The Gandhi-Irwin Pact, signed on March 5th, 1931, was a defining moment of the Indian Freedom Movement. This pact was negotiated over a span of many sittings and meetings between Mahatma Gandhi and the Viceroy, Lord Irwin.

The last of these meetings was held at the Delhi Gymkhana Club, which was known as the Imperial Delhi Gymkhana Club at the time. The Gandhi-Irwin Pact called an end to the Civil Disobedience Movement and guaranteed the release of all political prisoners. However, it was criticised for not having guaranteed the release of Revolutionaries Bhagat Singh, Azad and Rajguru.

The room where the last negotiation was held is now the Bridge room. Most members are blissfully unaware of the history behind their favourite meeting room.

Gandhiji with Lord Irwin

Photo Credits: Better India.com

29

Squirrel at the First Table

Our animal friends and pets play an important role in our lives, often as family members.

This story is about a much smaller animal, a squirrel that lived in the Rashtrapati Bhawan between 1946-47 with India's last Viceroy and first Governor General. Yes, this squirrel lived as a pet with Viceroy Mountbatten and his family.

The squirrel was notorious for running across the Rashtrapati Bhawan and finding her place at the dining table, where she would eat from the Viceroy's plate along with her human family.

This had never happened before and probably has never happened since.

Lord Mountbatten

Photo Credits: Pinterest

30

Mistaken Identity

'The whole campaign was a case of mistaken identity.'
–George McGovern

One of the most famous cases of mistaken identity was the assassination of Lord O'Dwyer, by Indian revolutionary Udham Singh. Udham Singh was a young man from Amritsar who witnessed his entire family perish at the Jallianwala Bagh massacre, at the hands of General Dyer.

Seeking revenge, Udham Singh prepared to assassinate General Dyer in London. He did assassinate a man at Westminster and was arrested and hanged for the act.

Later, it was found that the man he had killed was O'Dwyer, the Governor of Amritsar during the massacre in 1919, not General Dyer.

However, karma returned and General Dyer died an unrecognised, unknown man, years later.

Michael O' Dwyer
Photo Credits: Wikipedia

General Dyer
Photo credits: Wikipedia

31

The Unpaid Bill

Winston Churchill, the greatest Prime Minister of England once said:

"Never was so much owed by so many to so few."

He excelled at the English language and worked tirelessly to motivate the troops deployed at the front lines. However, when it came to payment of his own debts, he was never punctual.

A prime example of this is the still outstanding club bill, that can be seen till today inside the main building of the Bengaluru club.

Carefully preserved and displayed in a showcase, is an iconic unpaid bill of none other than Sir Winston Churchill. It is now an important part of history at the club. The amount was a princely sum of Rs. 13/- though today it could be called loose change!

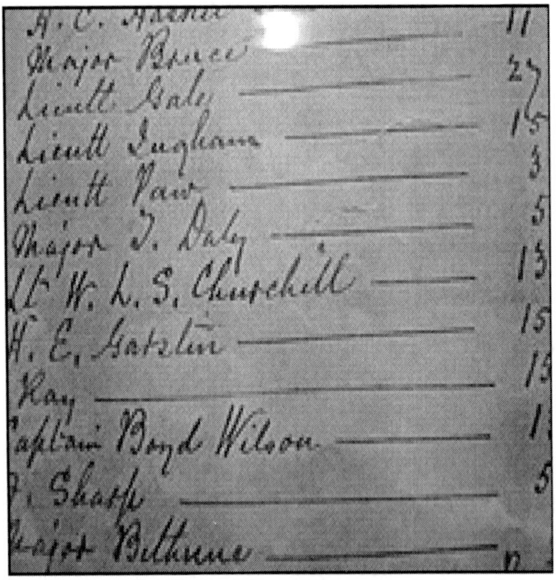

Churchill's unpaid bill

Photo credits: BBC

32

Alexander Invaded India

'Diplomacy is the art of telling people to go to hell in such a way that they ask for directions.' – ***Winston Churchill***

Greece was the cradle of democracy and India was the cradle of civilisation. They faced off at the Battle of the Hydaspes, when Alexander invaded India and established the Indo-Greek period of Ancient History in 352 BCE.

Centuries later, the Greek King Constantine II, came to India on a state visit.

It is believed that the then President Dr. S. Radhakrishnan, said to the visiting King. "You are the first Greek to have come by invitation. Alexander the Great visited India uninvited."

33

Races

'Wimbledon is getting a bit too much like Royal Ascot. It's not what happens or who wins, so much as what clothes do I have on.'
– *David Lloyd*

The Royal Ascot is an annual equestrian event that features both, the best-groomed horses, and the aristocratic high society of England. This is one event that also dictates the fashion trends of the year.

This reported incident occurred during the state visit of the President of India, Dr. S. Radhakrishnan, to the United Kingdom. This was a summer visit. The Queen was at her Balmoral Castle Residence in Scotland for the summer.

In order to honour the visiting dignitary, the Queen organised a charted train for the Indian President and his retinue to join her and the royal family at Balmoral. Her Majesty welcomed him at the Balmoral Castle station.

On seeing the Queen, who was dressed in a bright floral A-line dress, Dr. S. Radhakrishnan said, "My dear lady you look dressed for the races!" And patted her on the shoulders.

The Queen, 38 years younger than the President, was taken aback by such light-hearted conversation.

She had never been spoken to in that manner since acceding the crown in 1947, much less been patted on the shoulders by anyone other than her father, since the reigning sovereign is considered sacred.

President Radhakrishnan and Queen Elizabeth

Photo Credits: Age Foto Stock

34

Shoe Lace

'Truth, Beauty, Goodness and Love are as much structures of the Evolutionary Universe as the Sun and the Earth and the Moon.' – ***Jan Smuts***

Jan Smuts was a close confidant of Winston Churchill. He was the leader of the Pretoria regime in South Africa that legalised apartheid.

At the Tolstoy Farm in Johannesburg, South Africa, Mahatma Gandhi and other resistance leaders worked against these segregationist efforts of the government.

However, in 1913, the resistance movement in South Africa lost its most vocal supporter in Mahatma Gandhi, when he returned to serve India and her people.

Before leaving for India, Gandhiji sought an appointment with Jan Smuts, due to whom he had been arrested on more than one occasion.

At the meeting, rather than criticising Smuts for his actions, Gandhiji gave him a small gift as a farewell gesture. This gift was a pair of hand knitted slippers.

Years later, on the assassination of Mahatma Gandhi in 1948, Jan Smuts paid tribute to the Mahatma by wearing the same slippers Gandhi had knitted and presented to him before leaving Africa in 1913.

Reporters asked him to identify the slippers as the ones that the Mahatma had knitted. To this, Jan Smuts said, 'Yes, these are the slippers gifted to me by Mahatma Gandhi though I don't think myself fit to even tie his shoe laces'.

General Jan Smuts and Mahatma Gandhi

Photo Credits: Moral Upbringing Blog

35

Juggad Technology

For those of us living in North India, 'Juggad' is more than making the best of limited resources, or finding a way out. It can be termed as a lifestyle illustrated by the anecdote that follows.

This incident relates to the state visit of US President Bill Clinton and his daughter Chelsea Clinton to India. They travelled with 'The Beast,' a Cadillac Fleetwood.

During a preparatory run on Delhi roads, The Beast broke down and wouldn't move beyond the Red Fort. The Secret Service Detail on duty took the car to the nearest car repair workshop.

The shop assistant, a young boy, called the head mechanic from inside the workshop. The head mechanic asked the security men to not watch his actions, but to return after the car was fixed.

The mechanic then took a hammer and hit certain parts of the engine. In less than 10 minutes, the mechanic grinned at the Secret Service Detail and said, *"Juggad Hogaya! Ab issko kuch nahi hoga."*

(The car has been fixed! Now nothing will happen to it.)

On returning to USA, Bill Clinton had the opportunity of welcoming the Indian Prime Minister, Atal Bihari Vajpayee as a gesture of reciprocity. The Indian Prime Minister asked what is it that India might offer USA as part of their friendship. Bill Clinton responded by saying, "*Give us Juggad Technology.*" In response to this, the Indian Prime Minister said that *Juggad Technology* was a well-guarded state secret that could not be exchanged as it would put him and his government in India in jeopardy. It was *Juggad* that had held all the allies of the first National Democratic Alliance (NDA) together as a part of 'Pragmatic Politics'.

Bill Clinton and Prime Minister Atal Bihari Vajpayee at the Rashtrapati Bhawan, New Delhi

Photo Credits: India Today

Atal Bihari Vajpayee and Bill Clinton at the White House, Washington

Photo Credits: Nai Dunia

36

Maun-vrat Mondays

> *'At the stroke of the midnight hour, when the world sleeps, India shall awake to life and freedom. A moment comes, which comes, but rarely in history, when we step out from the old into the new, when an age ends, when the soul of a nation, long suppressed finds utterance.'*
>
> – ***Jawaharlal Nehru***

These are the iconic lines from the speech, 'Tryst with Destiny'. The phrase, 'Tryst with Destiny' was later picked up as the title of a book by Dominique Lapierre and Larry Collins. In order to research this book, the authors travelled to each key player in the quest for India's Independence. The main protagonist of the book was Lord Louis Mountbatten, a meticulous and organised gentleman.

Lord Mountbatten had a vast and organised library. In this extensive library, was a drawer filled with used envelopes that had a scrolled handwriting on the unused side.

When the authors asked Lord Mountbatten about those envelopes and their significance, the Lord responded that these envelopes were priceless as they were his conversations with Mahatma Gandhi.

With an inquisitive look the authors questioned Lord Mountbatten about the written conversations. Lord Mountbatten explained:

> On Mondays, the Mahatma observed abstinence from conversation with visitors.

Therefore, I (Lord Mountbatten) would only visit on Mondays. This allowed an uninterrupted and recorded conversation.

Lord and Lady Mountbatten with Gandhiji at the Viceregal House.

Photo Credits: Telegraph

37

Prime Minister, Not Madam

'What's in a name, a rose by any other name would smell just as sweet.'
– ***William Shakespeare***

My grandfather always narrates this story with a glint in his eye and this quote. It is, in his words, about two people whose lives and work we both admire, both as pioneers in their fields and as leaders. One in the military and the other, the first and till date, the only female Prime Minister of India.

A famous story about Sam (Field Marshal Sam Manekshaw) circulating in South Block before the Indo-Pak war was about Sam's habit of addressing Indira Gandhi as 'Prime Minister' instead of 'Madam', which was how most senior bureaucrats addressed her. After a briefing session with the Prime Minister, Sam and the group of Secretaries met in the Cabinet Secretary's office to discuss the inputs required for the defence forces for the impending war.

During the discussion, one of the Secretaries remarked about the rather odd practice Sam followed while addressing Mrs. Gandhi.

Sam's reply that, in the school he attended, his English teacher taught the students that the term 'Madam' denotes a lady in charge of a house of ill-fame and he has too high a regard for the Prime Minister to address her by that nom-de-plume. This reply left the bureaucrats speechless.

Sam Manekshaw and Indira Gandhi

Photo Credits: Times Now

38

The Country owes a Debt of Gratitude to him

'A 'yes' man is a dangerous man. He is a menace. He will go very far, he can become a minister, a secretary or a field marshal. He will never be a leader not respected, used by superiors, disliked by colleagues, despised by subordinates. So, discard the 'Yes' Man.'
– Sam Manekshaw

In the twilight years of his life, Sam Manekshaw was a man the government had completely neglected. Due to his ill health, he was admitted to the Willingdon Hospital in Tamil Nadu.

The then President of India, Dr. A.P.J. Abdul Kalam, went to visit Field Marshal Manekshaw prior to his demise. At this critical juncture, he requested the hospital staff to take proper care of the Field Marshal, as the nation owed a debt of gratitude to him.

This debt of gratitude was the victory in the war of 1971, that divided Pakistan and birthed a new nation on the map of the world: Bangladesh.

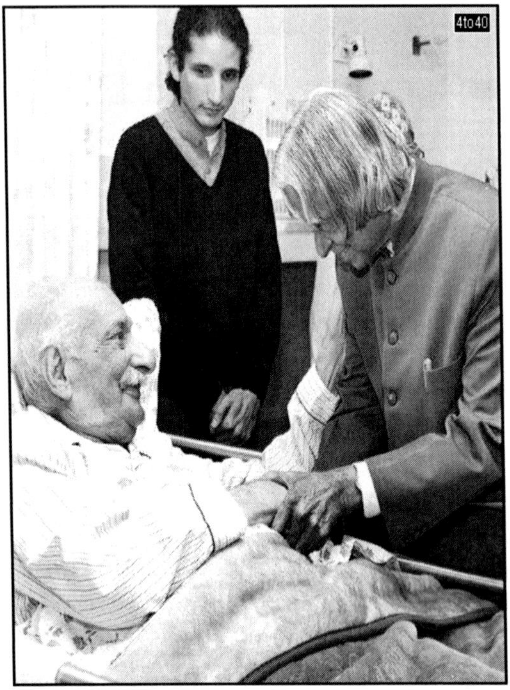

A.P.J. Abdul Kalam and Sam Manekshaw at Willingdon Hospital

Photo Credits: 4 to 40

39

Paid me in Half a Country

An old German proverb says: He who is quick to borrow is slow to pay.

Another story related to the life of Field Marshal Sam Manekshaw is a story of trade with Pakistan's General Yahya Khan.

Prior to independence from the British rule, Yahya Khan had bought Sam Manekshaw's red motorcycle and promised to pay his dues upon reaching Pakistan.

Due to the hurly burly of Partition of India in 1947, the General forgot the payment for purchase of the motorcycle.

Years later, in 1971 when Manekshaw was the Army Chief during the Bangladesh war and subsequent surrender of Pakistan, Manekshaw remembered this promise and is reported to have said, "Yahya Khan had promised to pay me for my motorcycle on reaching Pakistan. He never did and today, he has paid me in half a country."

Surrender of Pakistan, Creation of Bangladesh

Photo Credits: Outlook

40

Are Your Lordships in Consultation?

'A jury consists of twelve persons chosen to decide who has the better lawyer.' – ***Robert Frost***

This is an amusing short anecdote about Muhammad Ali Jinnah as a practicing lawyer. Jinnah was supposed to be an extremely passionate and vocal barrister.

On a particular day, he was arguing the facts of the case in a very systematic manner when suddenly, he noticed that the judge was playing with his pet dog's ear. Jinnah felt insulted by the judge's behaviour as he felt that the judge was not focussing on his arguments. Therefore, he stopped mid-sentence to draw the judge's attention.

During the duration of this pause, the judge enquired the reason for his pause. Jinnah curtly replied, "I thought your lordships (you and your dog) were in consultation regarding the judgement of this case."

The humiliated judge instantly began listening to Jinnah's arguments with undivided attention. However, he was determined to avenge this insult. The judge got his opportunity in a few hours.

In the evening, during the hearing, a donkey began braying outside the court house. The Judge then requested Jinnah to please resume his arguments the next day as he could not hear two donkeys braying at the same time!

41

The Perils of Devilling

'Good lawyers know the law; great lawyers know the judge.'
– ***Anonymous***

F.E. Smith, a renowned barrister of the 1920s era, who rose to become the Lord Chancellor of Justice of England and the first Earl of Birkenhead, was known for his scathing wit.

He once appeared in a sessions court in a contempt of court case to defend a young lawyer, moved by his fervent plea to protect him.

The young lawyer, who was devilling with a senior counsel, put his heart and soul in preparing for a case in which he was asked by his senior to appear independently.

He however, lost the case and as he was leaving, the court, the judge who passed him by, asked what he thought of the judgement. The young lawyer sullenly replied, "Very Disappointed." This offended the judge, who issued him a show cause notice the next day for Contempt of Court.

Barrister Smith, who appeared in the court on behalf of the young lawyer, argued brilliantly, quoting chapter and verse of law to convincingly establish that no contempt of court had been committed and in conclusion he added:

> "My Lord, he is but a young lawyer with little experience. Had he my experience of your lordship's judgements, he would never have been surprised at any of Your Lordship's judgement."

The contempt notice was quashed and the young lawyer was exonerated honourably.

F.E. Smith

Photo Credits: Wikipedia

42

Metre Gauge Body, Broad Gauge Brain

The advent of the railway system in India almost synchronised with the Mutiny of 1857, also known as India's first War of Independence.

Keeping in view the uprising of 1857 that nearly threw the British out of the country, the British rulers had deviously planned a three-pronged railway system for India. It consisted of broad-gauge, metre-gauge and narrow-gauge systems, measured by the width of the railway track. The broad gauge trains could ply on tracks of 5ft 6in width in the British ruled Central India.

The 600 odd Princely States were provided with the metre gauge system (tracks of 3ft 3.5in width) ensuring that they could not transgress to Central India.

The three hill stations of Shimla, Darjeeling and Ootacamand would be served by narrow-gauge trains (tracks measuring 2ft 6inches).

Many of the Princely States were foisted with British General Managers of their respective railways. The Jodhpur State Railways had an Englishman, Major Gordon, as the manager. His singular mission was to ensure that all trains under his control ran on time. As he lived in a bungalow close to the rail track, the engine drivers bringing the trains to Jodhpur would spot him standing on his lawn looking at his wrist watch to see if the trains were steaming in on time. He even introduced a reward system to motivate the drivers.

Major Gordon was a short man of about 4ft10inches. Because of his short stature, his compatriots bestowed on him the sobriquet of the 'Man with the metre-gauge body and broad-gauge brain.'

The British very adroitly managed to secure the support of the Princes by providing them exclusive and luxuriously appointed Railway Saloons for their personal travel.

After India's Independence and the abolition of Princely perks, the State Railways were merged to form the Indian Railways.

In 1980, these saloons came in handy to form one of the world's most luxurious train known as the 'Palace on Wheels Tourist Train'.

43

Will this Cheque Bounce?

In this last story, for this volume it would be fitting to describe the wit and humour of Field Marshal Manekshaw while receiving his last pension.

Field Marshal Manekshaw was not receiving his pension as the highest ranking Army Officer in the nation. President Dr. A.P.J. Abdul Kalam was extremely disturbed by this and visited the Field Marshal personally, in order to give him the cheque of his pension.

Upon seeing the sum on the cheque, Field Marshal Manekshaw asked the President with a glint in his eyes, "Are you sure that this cheque will not bounce?" Dr. A.P.J. Abdul Kalam reassured the Field Marshal with a smile and returned to Delhi.

References

Bibliography

1. Freedom at Midnight – Larry Collins and Dominique La Pierre
2. One Life is not Enough- K. Natawar Singh
3. Nehru: A Political Michaell Brecher
4. India After Gandhi- Ramchandra Guha
5. Treasury of Poems- Compilation
6. Field Marshal Sam Manekshaw- The Man and his Times by M.Panthaki and Zenobia Panthaki
7. Non Alignment Pact- India, Egypt, Yugoslavia, Ghana, Indonesia UN Charter, 1945
8. My Years with Indira Gandhi- P.C. Alexander
9. Indira Gandhi: India's Most Powerful Prime Minister- Sagarika Ghosh
10. Last 1000 days of the British Raj- Peter Clarke
11. Delhi Durbar- India International Centre, Occasional Publication
12. Empire of the Great Mughal- Annemarie Schimmel
13. India's China War- Neville Maxwell
14. Eagles over Bangladesh
15. Beyond the Lines - Kuldip Nayar
16. Between the Lines - Kuldip Nayar

Treaty of Versailles- Victors of World War I

Online Sources

Britannica website

BBC website

Al Jazeera Website

United Nations General Assembly Website

Photo Credits

(Not chapter-wise)

1. Wikipedia
2. Outlook
3. 4 to 40
4. Times Now
5. The Telegraph
6. Nai Dunia
7. India Today
8. Free Press Journal
9. Age Foto Stock
10. Unofficial Royalty
11. BBC
12. Scoop Whoop Café
13. Pinterest
14. Better India
15. Dawn.com
16. The Quint
17. National Gallery of London
18. Russian Council
19. Creative Commons
20. Historic Image outlet
21. Cysaby.com
22. Palace on Wheels website
23. Daily Hunt.com
24. Shutter Stock

25. Times of India
26. Quora
27. The Hindu
28. Amazon.com
29. Getty Images
30. Medium website
31. Amazon e-commerce website
32. Wikimedia
33. Hindustan Times
34. Reddit
35. Alamy stock

Short Biographies

Short Biographies of personalities whose quotes lend life to the beginning of the chapters-

1. Woodrow Wilson- He was the 28th President of the United States of America during the First World War. His term in office was between 1913-21. He is one of the architects of the Treaty of Versailles.
2. Andre Gide-A Nobel Laureate, French author and a Nobel Prize winner (Literature) (22 November, 1869—19 February 1951) with an aristocratic lineage. Many of his works have been converted into acclaimed films.
3. Roger A Caras- Born on May 28, 1928 was an American wildlife photographer, conservationist and television personality.
4. Amir Khusro- He was a court poet during the Qutub Dynasty. He is credited with the invention of Qawwali Music, Indian and Iranian music and the creation of the tabla and sitar.
5. Elizabeth Taylor- She was an acclaimed Hollywood actress known for her larger than life portrayal of Queen Cleopatra in the movie 'Anthony and Cleopatra' based on Shakespeare's play of the same name.
6. Noam Chomsky- was born in 1928. He revolutionised learning by treating language uniquely as a part of cognitive learning.
7. Billy Graham- He was born in Florida (USA) in 1918. He was an evangelist who spread his message through his preaching.

8. Mahatma Gandhi- He was born in 1869. He created a new method of protest called 'Satyagraha'. At the end of this, he with his mass support helped oust the British colonial rule from India.
9. Kamal- Kamal was a fictional maharaja who was the villain in the movie Octopussy.
10. Winston Churchill- He was the Prime Minister of Great Britain and Ireland during World War II. He was one of the architects of the United Nations and a leading diplomat amongst world leaders.
11. Jawaharlal Nehru- He was the first Prime Minister of Independent India, an architect of the Non-Aligned Movement and one of the leaders of the Independence Movement of India.
12. Napoleon Bonaparte- He was a military commander and general in the French Army. He is best known for the Napoleonic wars that were a catalyst in the enlightenment of Europe.
13. Sylvester MacNutt III- He is an author, podcast host and YouTube personality. He is also a motivational speaker.
14. Ashoka Madhavan- He was the editor of the Times of India during the National Emergency, who anonymously printed the obituary of Democracy.

Epilogue

It is said that time and tide wait for none. As said in the 'Brook' by Alfred Lord Tennyson, 'Time flows lower and lower to meet the sea.'

It happened yet again, the century changed, 20th became 21st. In 2020, the world stood at a threshold that no one had expected to see. It affected every aspect of our life.

It permanently changed the way humans interacted with each other, lifestyle management and conducting business. It was reminiscent of the year 1918, at the end of World War I, which brought with it political, social and cultural changes. The Ottoman Empire had broken down. Britain was the largest colonial master, upon which, as E.M. Forster once wrote, the 'sun never set'.

This brings me to another story, the story of how the Spanish flu of 1919 came to India. The current pandemic forces me to retell that tale.

'The World must be made a safe place for democracy.'

- Woodrow Wilson

With the noble intention of preventing another war, the allied and associated powers made a pact with Germany, one for lasting peace. They decided to sign the Treaty of Versailles and include a representative of each of the colonies, thus recognising their sizable contribution to the war effort.

A distinguished Maharaja, a former Chancellor of the Chamber of Princes from the State of Bikaner, India, was selected to represent the British colony. At this time, the Spanish flu of

1918-19 was traveling through Europe. An unintended fallout of the Maharaja's effort of escorting surviving Indian soldiers back to India, to be re-united with their families, was to bring along the dreaded influenza pandemic to the shores of India. What ensued was hardship and chaos with each passing day, increasing the number of crosses on the wall of the village chief's house to mark the number of deaths.

In that experience a century ago, there lay a message, one of cooperation and hope, that still rings true to this day, on an increasingly turbulent global stage.